WOMEN MANAGER_.

THE UNTAPPED RESOURCE

National Economic Development Office
Royal Institute of Public Administration

This report has been prepared for publication by the Manpower Division of the National Economic Development Office (NEDO) in collaboration with the Royal Institute of Public Administration (RIPA). It is based upon a research survey commissioned from the Institute of Manpower Studies (IMS) and carried out by Wendy Hirsh and Charles Jackson. Employer best practice case-study research was also undertaken by Duarte Figueira (NEDO) and Angela Payne (RIPA).

The National Economic Development Council (NEDC) brings together representatives of Government, management, the trade unions and other interests to assess economic performance and opportunities for improving it. The NEDC meets quarterly, under the chairmanship of the Chancellor of the Exchequer and other Secretaries of State.

There are 18 sector groups and working parties covering different parts of industry or working on practical industrial issues.

The National Economic Development Office supports the work of the Council and its sector groups and working parties. It carries out independent research and provides advice on ways of improving economic performance, competitive power and the efficiency of industry, stimulating new ideas and practical action.

ISBN 07494 0416 7

© Crown Copyright 1990

Published by Kogan Page Ltd
120 Pentonville Road
London N1 9JN
in association with
National Economic Development Office,
Millbank Tower Millbank,
London SW1P 4QX

November 1990

CONTENTS

PREFACE

One of the most important responsibilities of a chief executive is to appoint the right senior managers and to ensure that there are others being developed to succeed them. Managerial talent is always in demand and perpetually in short supply. Employers who maximise the use of their managerial potential gain a competitive advantage or, in the case of the public sector, are able to provide a more efficient and effective service.

For whatever reason, you may call it culture, lack of imagination or sheer prejudice, employers under-utilise female managerial potential. Perhaps one in a hundred top managers in the UK is a woman, a figure which rises to an estimated 4 per cent of senior and middle managers. Since there is no reason to believe that women are less ambitious or talented than men, these figures are evidence of a vast waste of ability. This report attempts to explain why this should be so and what chief executives can do about it. It emphasises that steps like career breaks and objective promotion procedures may not be enough. What is required is more basic - a shift based on taking a new look at management careers. Too often, corporate expectations of managers that may not reflect real organisational needs inhibit women's career progress.

At BP we aim to offer all employees a challenging career in a non-discriminatory setting. Perhaps more important, we encourage employees to strike a balance between home and work. We believe that such an approach helps recruit and retain talented women and allows them to develop their full managerial potential. Like all employers, we still have a long way to go. However, we have no doubts about the advantages to be gained.

Robert Horton
Chairman
British Petroleum

FOREWORD

The low proportion of women in management in the United Kingdom has become an issue of concern and many of the reasons for their under–representation are becoming clear. While some employers have improved opportunities for women managers, few have given the issue a high priority. There are now additional reasons why forward looking employers should address this question.

Managers at all levels are becoming a significant proportion of those who work in the UK. Between 1981 and 1988 the number of corporate managers and administrators increased by over 110,000 and projections indicate that numbers will grow still more rapidly in the next decade. This in part reflects the general trend towards higher skill levels throughout our society and economy.

The magnitude of the change taking place makes it imperative that the supply of managers is of sufficient quality. Underlying talent and potential is equally divided between the sexes, and in some occupations and professions a few women are actually being appointed to the more senior positions. It is important that we should take full advantage of the talents of women in senior management. A failure to use their managerial talents, which are testified to by the individual success stories with which we are all becoming familiar, would prove a serious loss to the UK. For women, the cost would take the form of a frustration of their ambitions.

This report is aimed at helping organisations to develop career structures which are capable of seeking out and bringing forward the best managerial skills available. It provides a framework within which employers may identify why they are failing to realise that potential and it provides pointers for action to ensure that more women with ambition and talent become managers.

WALTER ELTIS
Director General
NEDO

DAVID FALCON
Director General
RIPA

WHY WE NEED MORE WOMEN MANAGERS

In the decade between 1973 and 1983 the giant
American communications firm American Telephone
and Telegraph (AT&T) discovered that it had neglected
managerial talent in half its workforce. The company
employed 120,000 staff, half of whom were female.
However, very few women were to be found in the
higher reaches of the occupational structure. In order to
respond to a charge of discrimination made by the US
Equal Employment Opportunity Commission, the
company opened its assessment centre to all its junior
women managers. It discovered that 40 per cent had
further management development potential. These
women were then placed by AT&T on career
advancement programmes to develop their managerial
expertise in a number of different company functions.
Up to that point women managers had tended to be
concentrated in certain functions only.

A decade later the results were clear. The proportion of
women middle managers had increased from one in
seventy to one in seven.

Widening options – opening management opportunities for women

The AT&T example illustrates what a number of similar
studies and examples have demonstrated many times.
Employers are largely content to fish for managerial
talent in only half the available pool. This is a waste of
managerial potential and competitive advantage which
must be addressed.

This report could not be more timely. In the 1990s employers will not only need better managers, they will need more managers. A forecast from the Institute for Employment Research (IER) in 1989 estimates that the number of corporate managers and administrators is likely to grow by 450,000 between 1988 and the year 2000. The total number of all types of managers is projected to increase by around 700,000. In addition, the effect of the Single European Market and, indeed, the increasing level of international competition will place unprecedented demands on managers. Companies with good managers will flourish.

The next few years will be critical for the role of women in the workplace. Young women are becoming increasingly well-educated and well-qualified. They are often strong team players and, given the opportunities, are able leaders, with greater ambition and career expectations than employers give them credit for.

But, although women already make up 45 per cent of the labour force, few play a part in management. An optimistic estimate, defining management in the broadest possible way, is that perhaps one in four of all managers is a woman. At higher levels, according to the British Institute of Management, perhaps four per cent of middle and senior managers are women, falling to one or two per cent at senior executive levels. Figures indicate that in the USA more women become managers at lower levels but women are still poorly represented in middle and senior executive posts. Given that there is no evidence that women as a whole have poorer aptitudes for management jobs, this is in one sense surprising. But surely no one has any illusions about the causes.

Management careers – beyond reach

Women are poorly represented in management for two reasons. First, they find the climb to the top tougher than men. Many fail to get on the right track to promotion and may be disadvantaged by their employers' selection and promotion procedures.

Second, for historical reasons, management jobs have developed in ways which also keep out many women. A visitor from Mars would be forgiven for thinking that they have been specifically designed for men married to full-time wives and mothers who shoulder the burden of family life. This support enables such men to cope with the long hours and dedication that management careers demand.

In the 1970s top management might have asked – "why change?". The system had been tried and tested. But in the much more competitive 1990s they cannot continue to ignore the managerial talents of over half the population. In any case, in the 1990s, the picture of family life relied on by this pattern of management careers is increasingly untypical. Families have changed and so have attitudes. There are more one-parent families, more families headed by women and fewer supported by full-time wives and mothers. Women work and have greater career expectations than ever before. Not all will want to be top managers. But those who do and who have the talent ought to be given better opportunities to fulfil their potential.

Men's attitudes may be changing too. Management careers take a high toll, placing considerable pressure on health, time and families. Without a full-time wife at home, the strain increases. One survey has suggested that men are becoming "reluctant managers" - reluctant to strive for career success at the expense of personal relationships. It may be going too far to suggest that the supply of potential male managers may contract; however, if succession planning is taken seriously by top managers, these dangers should not be ignored.

Moving ahead - two approaches

For employers who want to respond positively and profitably to the opportunity to realise the managerial talents of women, there are two approaches to consider.

Employers could simply leave management jobs as they are, but introduce ways of making a full-time managerial career and family life easier for women (and men) to combine. Subsidised childcare or workplace nurseries would be important steps in this direction. Women could also be helped by opening access to management training and revised recruitment procedures. But although this approach may attract or retain more women in the workforce, it is unlikely, on its own, to significantly improve women's access to management.

The second approach, which would ease the path for women into management would lead, over time, to much more dramatic solutions, based on a radical and fundamental rethink of employers' attitudes to management careers. It acknowledges that women, and increasingly men, want career success but not at the expense of their family lives. It also acknowledges that the time has come to create a new photofit picture for tomorrow's manager, in which gender is an irrelevance and ability and potential are the only criteria for career success.

Improving women's access to management careers is a matter of urgency. What's at stake is whether employers can find, within a changing workforce, the best managers available.

This report aims to help employers in that search. The issues covered include:

▲   The use made of the managerial potential of women in the UK workforce.

▲   How employees become managers.

▲   Why women are less likely to be promoted than men

▲   The factors affecting the development of women's managerial careers.

▲   What employers are doing to encourage women into management.

The chapter called "Time for a rethink" describes the broad policy alternatives facing employers keen to make better use of women's talents.

Finally, a checklist for employers is provided. This details the questions which should be addressed in seeking to improve the access of women to management careers.

WOMEN MANAGERS TODAY

No matter which survey you look at, no matter what measure you take, fewer women than men are to be found in management in the UK at all levels. From the most junior manager to the most senior board level director, men outnumber women; and the further up the hierarchy you go, the fewer women you'll find. In the US, by comparison, the number of female managers tripled during the seventies and by the late eighties women made up 38 per cent of managers, although, there too, most were to be found at junior management levels. This suggests that in the UK the managerial talents of women are largely untapped.

Broadly defined, there may be up to three million managers in the UK. According to the most recent Labour Force Survey, 27 per cent are women. Of the million or so middle or senior managers in the UK, perhaps 4 per cent are women. At the top of UK industry, though, this general shortage turns into a drought. It is estimated that a mere 1 to 2 per cent of senior executive positions are held by women (Figure 1).

Estimates vary, depending upon the definition of a manager used within the firm, and the industry or occupational group being examined. A survey of 95 top CBI firms carried out for the Hansard Society Commission in 1989 revealed that women made up 6.7 per cent of senior managers. A second survey carried out

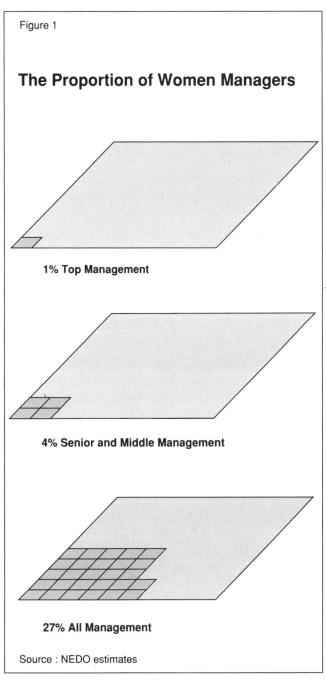

Figure 1

The Proportion of Women Managers

1% Top Management

4% Senior and Middle Management

27% All Management

Source : NEDO estimates

by the same body of 180 of the top 200 CBI firms revealed that women made up only 0.5 per cent of executive directors on the main boards of these companies. The survey also revealed that the number of women directors on subsidiary boards appeared to be increasing, albeit from a low base.

Even in sectors where women are well represented as employees in the UK, their managerial talents are not used. Nursing is a particularly graphic example. Over 90 per cent of qualified nurses are women but in 1985 46 per cent of chief officers, the most senior managers in health authorities, were men.

Similarly, nearly half the employees in the Civil Service are women. But most are to be found in the lower clerical grades. At "principal" level - the grade that is the gateway to senior posts - only eight per cent are women. A mere four per cent of employees who pass through this gateway and onto a higher managerial path are women.

A recent comprehensive survey of 1,000 women managers in local government shows that, despite a decade of equal opportunities legislation, women remain concentrated in lower level jobs. That so few women occupy top jobs in local government is a matter of acute concern, not least because local authorities are encouraged to see women as a solution to their future recruitment problems.One long term positive change in the structure of the UK economy which should have

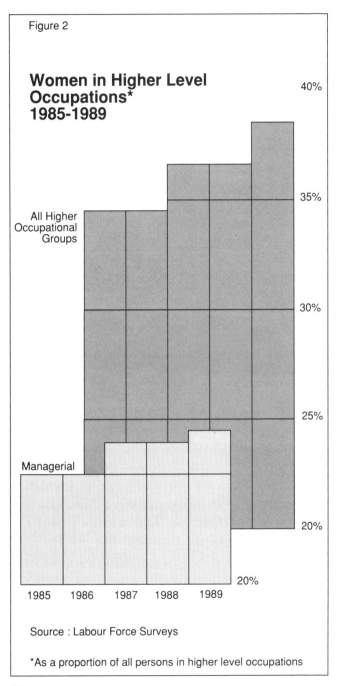

Figure 2

Women in Higher Level Occupations* 1985-1989

Source : Labour Force Surveys

*As a proportion of all persons in higher level occupations

been assisting women's climb up the corporate ladder is the decline of employment in the traditionally male-dominated manufacturing sector. This has been accompanied by a rise in employment in the female-dominated service sector. But despite these changes in women's favour, opportunities for women in management have not materialised. They are unlikely to improve without employer support and action.

Nearly 45 per cent of the UK's 22 million employees are women, but many are in jobs with less pay and less status than men. A lower proportion of women than men are professionals, employers and managers (Figure 2). A higher proportion of woman are to be found in junior non-manual and lower level manual jobs. This is especially true of part-time workers, of whom women form the vast majority. Women often return to a job of lower status and pay than the one they left. Women's talents are being under-utilised in the labour force, and the UK economy is poorer for this reason.

New opportunities for women

The role women play in the workforce will be particularly important over the next few years. Currently, it is estimated that about 90,000 people are appointed to their first management job each year, and there is widespread agreement that managers will be an increasingly important group of employees in the future (Figure 3).

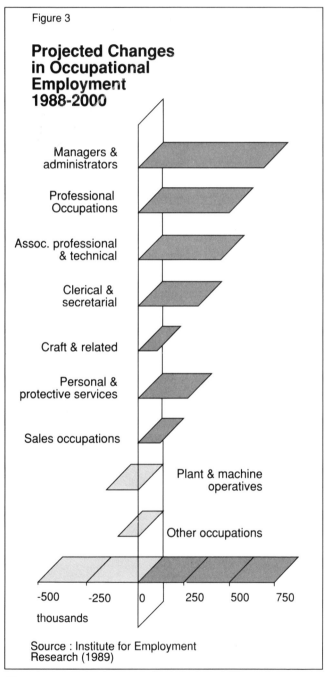

Figure 3

**Projected Changes
in Occupational
Employment
1988-2000**

Managers &
administrators

Professional
Occupations

Assoc. professional
& technical

Clerical &
secretarial

Craft & related

Personal &
protective services

Sales occupations

Plant & machine
operatives

Other occupations

-500   -250   0   250   500   750

thousands

Source : Institute for Employment
Research (1989)

As the number of young people entering the labour market will be lower in the nineties, women are expected to make up the shortfall. Nearly 95 per cent of the increase in the labour force up to 2000 may be made up by women. Yet there are signs that British women are not being encouraged develop to the full potential of their skills.

Only 55 per cent of British women in employment worked full time in 1989. Since part time work is often considered less meaningful than full time work, women with managerial potential in part time work are overlooked by employers.

At the same time women are improving their career prospects. Women gained 45 per cent of first degrees last year, though they are still substantially under-represented on many scientific and technical courses. The proportion of women on business and management courses has increased markedly in recent years. They make up approximately one third of university and almost half of polytechnic and college students on such courses. Women's participation in higher education has also been growing much faster than men's (Figure 4).

Demands from employers for highly qualified people, together with the drive for mutual recognition of professional and related qualifications in post 1992 Europe means that qualifications may become increasingly important in providing an entry pass into managerial jobs.

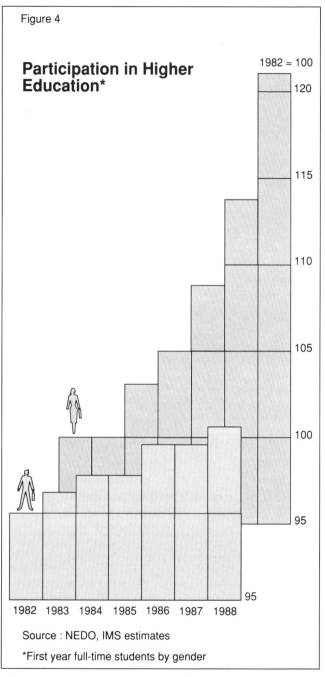

Figure 4

Participation in Higher Education*

1982 = 100

Source : NEDO, IMS estimates

*First year full-time students by gender

Employers need to recognise that this recent growth in the numbers of well qualified women increases the proportion of female potential in the pool of managerial talent. The real test for employers in the 1990s will be to capitalise on this resource as the demand for managers increases.

WHAT IT TAKES TO GET TO THE TOP

Ask a hundred managers how they got into management jobs and you'll probably get a hundred different answers. Routes into management differ from sector to sector; from employer to employer. But most managers' careers do share common characteristics from which a picture of the typical management career can be built. And the first requirement for success is to find the right track to promotion.

In Britain, management is not a job that most young aspirants enter straight from the education system. Only 12 per cent of UK managers have a first or higher degree. Fewer still have business or management qualifications. Promotion to management, and the responsibility for managing resources, including people, is awarded on the basis of perceived aptitude and experience. As well as gaining qualifications (and these are likely to become more important for entering management) women aspiring to management careers also need to build up relevant work experience.

Accumulating a track record

Usually, candidates are promoted into junior management from within a single function. So a good production line worker is promoted to production controller, or a good salesperson may become a junior sales manager.

That is not enough to get candidates into junior and middle management jobs, though. Senior management is often dominated by managers in general roles who have substantial experience of one or more of the functions perceived to be crucial or central to understanding the business. For example, sound knowledge of the production process is more likely to lead to promotion in a manufacturing company, whereas store management may well be the best path to promotion in a retail chain.

In some sectors, professional qualifications provide the typical passport into management. In the past most managers in banks have been asked to study for banking exams. And some professional qualifications, like accountancy, lead not just to a career in finance, but open the door to general business management.

Management training schemes are another route into management. Entry to these is generally confined to existing employees showing managerial potential, or to another specific target group, like graduates. As suggested in the previous chapter, although graduate entry into management has been limited in numbers in the past, an increasing number of employers expect graduates to provide the feedstock of middle and senior management in the future.

Getting the right qualifications and amassing the right experience is a start, but employers also expect their potential managers to fulfil other, often unspoken requirements. These are less to do with whether a candidate can do the job or not and more to do with whether they fit employers' expectations of what the typical manager should have achieved and how he or she should behave.

Continuous employment

Candidates striving for the top management jobs will usually need to show a good and continuous employment record. Experience in the early 1980s shows how difficult it is for male managers to find another management job after a period of unemployment. Employers fear that managers lose their confidence and their skills when they are out of work for even a short time. Broken periods of employment do not fit in with the normal managerial career.

High workload

But aspiring managers have to do more than demonstrate continuous employment. In the private sector, increasing competition at home and abroad has forced many companies to keep a tight rein on the number of managers employed and has raised expectations about the responsibility and workload that managers should handle. Top performing companies expect very strong commitment from their managers, often involving long hours and considerable stress. Work-related travel, and entertaining clients, as well as working at home, means that many managers put in at least a 12 hour day.

The 'right' age

Age is another factor that determines progression through organisations. Management careers are paced so that by the time managers reach senior level they still have a number of productive years before retirement. Often, those aiming for senior management are expected to have arrived by the time they are in their early forties. Obviously, this makes the thirties a critical career stage, in which managers muster as much varied experience as they can and demonstrate their senior management potential in a series of very demanding jobs.

Geographical mobility

To get the variety of experience senior management careers demand, there is a further expectation that managers must be mobile. Geographical mobility may be required by an employer, but, where promotion is blocked, ambitious managers may also want to move between one employer and another to progress their careers. Geographical mobility seems to be particularly important at middle management levels, and above, and for those on 'fast-track' schemes. The idea is that managers are exposed to a very broad range of job experience, perhaps in a number of countries.

Hurdling to the top

Finally, successful managers learn how to negotiate the hurdles that pave the way to promotion. Securing a

first-class report at appraisal time or turning in
satisfactory performances at interview boards may be
examples of how the more visible hurdles are cleared.
But there are also hidden hurdles to overcome.
Employers, knowingly or not, look for managers whose
faces fit their organisations.

In summary, then, the typical British manager starts off
in jobs, on training schemes or with qualifications
necessary for managerial promotion. He (and he usually
is a he) will have experience in functions seen as essential
to understanding the business, and will then move into a
more general role. He will be continuously employed,
work long hours, aim to reach senior management by 40
and be geographically mobile. He will also be a
successful hurdler in the promotion race.

Up to now, if women wanted to reach the top, this is
what they have had to do. In the past the chances that
they could meet these demands have been very slim. In
the promotion race, the odds have been against them
every step of the way.

PROMOTION HURDLES IN THE RACE FOR THE TOP

Finding the right track to promotion is crucial for runners in the race to the top. Understanding the hurdles as they presently exist is essential for employers who want to see more women in management.

Women's chances of even joining the race are often dramatically reduced by the early career choices they make. Jobs with poor career prospects, like secretarial, clerical and sales work, offer few opportunities for reaching management positions, yet all are the domain of women workers.

Where women do line up at the start of the race and take up higher status occupations and careers, they may still not get on the right track to promotion. This is because, more often than men, they get into jobs seen as support, rather than central, functions in the business.

Within insurance companies, for example, women are more likely to be personnel professionals than actuaries. Within retailing, they are more likely to handle staff management than store management. Within manufacturing, women are more likely to be in sales than production. Some functional differences can be excused by the low percentage of women with scientific and technical skills, but by no means all.

Promotion out of a support function is not easy. Employers argue that candidates with this type of background lack the real business understanding needed for senior or general management.

Employers also often expect - as we saw earlier - candidates for middle and senior management jobs to have experience of more than one business function. Women, however, seem to stay as specialists for longer than men, moving less frequently within a single employer and arriving later in generalist roles. Where men and women do reach the same managerial occupation, they will probably have travelled along different routes. An as yet unanswered question is: do women occupy certain roles and functions out of choice or because they cannot enter mainline managerial routes? As with so many aspects of this subject, cause and effect are hard to separate. Employers who do not recognise the talents of ambitious women, however, will probably lose them quickly. The practice of changing employers to achieve a promotion is more common among women than men.

The right track but a slower speed

Even when women find the right track to a management career, they still fail to be promoted as quickly or as frequently as men. Sometimes women have not received the right training. In banking, for example, a minority of women gain the professional qualifications necessary for a career in management. But women who start the promotion race with the same qualifications as men also gain advancement less rapidly.On management training schemes for graduates, men and women usually begin as equals, selected according to common criteria. And, except when a science degree is required, women often make up half or more of the entry intake. According to employers, female graduate trainees perform well. It might therefore be thought that, by now, a substantial cohort of women graduates who joined management training schemes in the late seventies would be entering middle management jobs. There is, however, little sign that these women are entering even junior management in substantial numbers.

Academic research has found that women fall behind men in their careers quite early - certainly far too early to put the blame on having children. Women graduates often have lower status jobs, more limited promotion prospects and earn significantly less than men. And the fact that women are badly represented on vocationally relevant courses like engineering and technology does not explain the disparity. No matter what academic course they followed, women graduates are, by and large, less successful in their careers than men.

These findings are true of both the public and private sectors. Women in the Civil Service also progress more slowly than men from the same entry points. Women do particularly badly in progressing through the main clerical grade, but fast track women trainees, too, are promoted more slowly than their male peers.Researchers have attempted to throw light on the problem by examining how employers' selection and promotion decisions disadvantage women. One study of British banks revealed that closed promotion systems, where jobs are not advertised internally, may cause inequity. It seems that personnel and line managers don't always have an accurate impression of women employees' career commitment or ambition.

A harder path

When women do reach senior management positions they have invariably had a harder time getting there. This is even the case in a career like nursing, where in total women substantially outnumber men.

One study shows that female chief nursing officers were promoted more slowly than men from the same level and had held a greater number of posts before promotion to management. This may be partly explained by the younger age of men in the sample who were the beneficiaries of recent attempts to speed up nursing careers. But it still does not explain why men climbed faster than women on the management ladder.

The research provides a fascinating example of the way in which a lack of 'centrality' in career experience does not inhibit male careers. Most of the women managers had started their careers in general nursing, the most central function in the health service. By contrast 60 per cent of male managers had come from the much less obviously central field of mental illness nursing.

Appearing not to be ambitious?

One of the assumptions often made about women is that they are not as ambitious as men or as career-oriented. But is this a fair interpretation of the evidence?

Analysing results from a British Institute of Management survey of women managers in the UK, researchers recently concluded that the view that women are less ambitious or career oriented than men appears to be little more than a popular myth. Other research indicates that career oriented women may well be even more ambitious and committed to their careers than many men. But, significantly for companies' human resource policies, women and men managers are often differently motivated. Intrinsic factors such as personal growth seems more important to women than extrinsic factors like pay and status.

In some occupations women seem more wary than men of applying for promotion. In the Civil Service, one of the few organisations where the promotion process is monitored, women below management levels appear hesitant about applying for promotion. This will pose serious problems for the future if more and more organisations switch over to self-development cultures where employees take charge of their own careers and apply for promotion on their own initiative. Alternatively, the encouragement of self-development and positive employer approaches to women managers could remove some of the inhibitions women feel about applying for promotion.Similarly, lack of support mechanisms may result in women turning down promotion opportunities. Data from the Northern Ireland Civil Service shows that where women are offered promotion, they are four times more likely than men to turn it down. It has been shown that, at lower grades, a requirement to change location on promotion is often the reason for refusal, while, at middle management level, a reluctance to change to different types of work, and concerns about the loss of part-time working options, appear more significant.

Other studies show women to be more career-minded than employers assume. A recent Institute of Manpower Studies (IMS) survey of a large sample of pharmacists found that 63 per cent of students were female but few women reach management positions. The study revealed a varying life cycle of career aspirations among female pharmacists. Women who had recently returned to work after having children were mainly concerned with the immediate problems of managing the demands of home and work. Older women, however, who had taken career breaks and had older children, showed a strong interest in career progression. Their managers, though, were not fully aware of these women's ambitions.

The trouble with examining the attitudes of women managers too closely, is that they are still a small and rare breed. And to break through against such strong odds may indeed require an unusual level of commitment and ambition. Women as a whole may well have a more ambivalent attitude towards career progression. The lesson to learn may be that women, like men, should not be regarded as invariably for or against promotion and management jobs. The attitude women adopt may vary at different points in their careers as well as depending upon the support available to them.

Attitudes that hinder and discriminate

One factor keeping women out of management is a belief that their management style differs from that displayed by men and that the male managerial style is the one that companies, knowingly or not. promote.

Although the evidence is not clear-cut, research indicates that women may well have a managerial style that is distinctive and different from men's. It is argued that women managers show greater concern for relationships and have better interpersonal skills. Other research conducted in 1987 found there to be few differences in relation to the managerial style and the job performance of men and women.

However, by promoting more male than female managers, employers probably create attitudinal barriers which inhibit women's promotion aspirations. These attitudes may seep into the criteria used in management selection and effectively build-in discrimination against women. Management, after all, is not a job for which the skills and knowledge required can be easily defined. The Management Charter Initiative, which is seeking to define managerial competence criteria, may help. Employers normally look for a combination of knowledge, skill and personal attributes, like the ability to lead and to motivate, which they believe make good managers. Many of the personal attributes sought by employers are very vague and an IMS study concluded in 1988 that the criteria for management are not just vague 'but also rather male'. Employers tend to highlight the dominant, assertive, decisive aspects of management behaviour and play down the team working and supportive behaviour. Such a conclusion may be controversial, but if correct would be important. Simply ignoring it could cost British employers dear in the future. Already researchers are warning that, as organisations become more skilled and more decentralised, tomorrow's manager will need to be less autocratic and better able to build and maintain relationships across the organisation and with those outside.

One consequence of using a male model of management is that few female role models exist. If there are so few women in management, then women will work surrounded by men. Their bosses will be men; the jobs they apply for will have been occupied by men. In these circumstances, a woman may be turned down for promotion simply because she doesn't fit the image left by the last male job holder.

Taking the prejudice out of promotion

Even when employers do not set criteria for management jobs which weigh against women applicants, the way candidates are assessed may allow discrimination to creep into the selection process. An interesting example is provided, once again, by the Civil Service.

Managers in the Civil Service are asked to rate the performance of their subordinates and also their potential for promotion. This assessment is entirely subjective and produces some fascinating results. Although women's scores are just as high as men for performance, when it comes to 'potential' their ratings lag behind. Since the 'potential' rating is taken very seriously by promotion boards, this is likely to be an important reason why women are promoted more slowly than men.

Even major UK employers do not make widespread use of selection methods, like psychological testing, which help to take the bias out of personnel decisions. Instead, they rely on subjective assessment methods like interviews. In this, British companies lag well behind their US counterparts, where psychological testing is acknowledged as an important way of minimising bias and achieving greater equality of opportunity. However, professional judgement is needed to use the tests and questionnaires fairly and users must recognise the limitations of these techniques.

Assessment centres are an increasingly popular way of selecting and appraising managers. As far as the elimination of bias is concerned, their strength is that candidates are set a series of exercises which simulate work tasks. Candidates therefore have the opportunity to demonstrate their skills to the assessor.

Again, care needs to be taken to ensure that assessors apply uniform criteria when making their judgements and to avoid the building of bias and sex-stereotyping into the assessment system.

THERE IS LIFE OUTSIDE MANAGEMENT

Even when they clear the promotion hurdles, aspiring women and men managers still have to obey certain behavioural rules if they are to reach the top. Long hours, continuous employment, significant geographical mobility and a series of highly challenging, testing jobs are the price employees pay for the nation's plum management positions.

These demands are taxing for men, but they pose particular problems for women because they clash so strongly with the existing division of domestic responsibilities. As a result, many conclude that combining a management career with family life is not an option open to them. To have a successful management career may well mean sacrificing too much of the time commitment of a family life. That is a price which men have not been asked to pay and most women have not been prepared to pay.

Analysis of data collected by a British Institute of Management membership survey in 1988 shows women managers are less likely to be married than their male peers and, if married, are less likely to have children. Only 58 per cent of women managers are married, compared with 93 per cent of men. Of those women who are married, only 52 per cent have children, compared to 89 per cent of men. So what is it about career and family that brings these two areas into conflict in women's lives, but complement one another in men's?

The answer lies both in the uneven distribution of domestic responsibilities and in the design of management careers. Marriage, or living with someone, even without children, can have a damaging effect on women's career opportunities, as researchers found in 1989 when they examined the impact of cohabitation and domestic responsibilities on graduate careers.

Within three years of graduation, over half the women in the study were married or living in permanent relationships and shouldering the major share of responsibility for household chores and, where appropriate, childcare. They also reported that they were more likely to give help to, rather than receive help from, their partners with work. Not surprisingly, three times as many women as men believed marriage had a negative impact on their career prospects.

Marriage may also restrict a woman's geographical mobility since women still tend to follow their husbands and partners. It may also reduce the importance of her career in the family's eyes. When researchers asked one group of male professionals and managers whether their own careers took precedence over their wives', 80 per cent said 'yes'. In contrast, under 15 per cent of women professionals and managers believed their careers took precedence. But 61 per cent of women and only 15.5 per cent of men thought both partner's careers to be of equal importance. Employers seeking to maximise their investment in women managers will need to ensure that these attitudes do not simply reflect the perceptions women have of their chances of progressing in their chosen careers.

Motherhood and managerial careers

Many women manage to successfully combine the early years of marriage or a permanent relationship and a career. It is when they become mothers that the real conflict hots up.

Motherhood clashes with management careers for two reasons. First, a dearth of good and flexible childcare facilities means that even women who want to return to work cannot find suitable childcare to cover the long hours that management careers demand. Second, for the majority of women who want to spend at least some daylight hours with their children, a full-time management career becomes almost impossible.

Few women take only the minimum statutory maternity leave. Some want to spend time with their young children, some can't find good, reasonably priced childcare and some find the strain of balancing home, children, husband and full-time work just too exhausting.

A family's childcare problems are not constant, but are changing and recurring. Both pre-school and school-age children present difficulties. Pre-school children need care during the full period while their parents are working and travelling while school-age children need care before and after school and during the school holidays. All children need extra care when they are sick or when, for some reason, existing childcare arrangements break down. As childcare is usually women's responsibility, they have to dovetail their own working day with that of their care arrangements. Employers often make no allowance for this. In fact, they may well interpret women's adherence to fixed hours as a lack of commitment. But women often can't elect to work longer hours because their partners already do and, they, therefore, cannot share the childcare burden.

If she is lucky, a woman manager may be able to combine time at home with a career by using a career-break scheme. Other women may try to work part-time, although part-time working is not usually a real option if they are hoping for promotion and a management career.

Many of the answers being developed by employers to these problems are described in the next chapter. The first step employers can take is to acknowledge that the normal pattern of managerial work is impracticable for women seeking to juggle childcare and other responsibilities, however highly committed they may be.

Caring for the elderly

In addition, it can no longer be assumed, once childcare responsibilities have declined, that caring duties are finished altogether.

While the country's pool of young people is shrinking, the number of elderly people has been increasing - both in absolute terms and as a proportion of the population. It has been projected that the number of people aged 65 and over will increase by over a million during the next 20 years, to about 9.5 million or 16 per cent of the total population.

An increase in the number of people requiring care in the community, bolstered by government preference for the care of the elderly, sick and disabled within the community rather than in institutions, has been accompanied by a reduction in the pool of people available to provide it.

Family size has declined, as has the number of single women who, in the past, have been traditional careers. Greater geographical mobility also means that people are less likely to have relatives living nearby. Such factors suggest that the task of caring will fall more heavily on fewer people. Already, one adult in seven now provides regular care to someone who is sick, elderly or disabled, and the majority of these carers are women. These trends are likely to affect both the supply of women workers and the hours they can work. Employers will need to be more flexible in their use of women (and men) with elderly care responsibilities, in the same way as those with child care commitments.

Pacing the modern managerial career

Whatever compromise is arranged, women's careers are stunted when they stop working full time. And, as women's careers slow down, male managers are moving quickly up the managerial ladder.

We saw earlier that the thirties is a make or break period in the life of ambitious managers. It is also a time of high stress and mobility. If women have their children in their early thirties then they do so at the most critical time for career development. If they have their children young and try for a career in their late twenties, other managers believe they are too old to become trainees.

Women are also rejected on the grounds of age if they try to return to work in their forties after child-rearing. However they play it, they lose out. The pacing of a modern managerial career could not be a worse challenge for women attempting to combine work with family life.

In fact, when women return to work they are likely to come back to a more junior job than they held before. Few employers give any recognition to the experience women acquire while running a home and managing a family, even though the organisational skills required are highly relevant to managerial work roles.

But if the pacing of managerial careers poses problems for women, it should be said it also poses problems for men. They are expected to have boundless energy and commitment at work at a time when they also have young families.

HELPING WOMEN ON THE ROAD TO MANAGEMENT

Few British employers have seriously tried to make the road to management as even for women as it is for men. And only a handful are exploring ways of reconciling the demands made on women at work and at home, or changing the attitudes which keep talented women out of the most challenging and best-paid jobs. This chapter describes the steps that some employers have taken so far to address women's needs at work and how effective these steps are likely to be in attracting women back to work and into management. It is not intended to be an exhaustive list of policies or initiatives, but a guide for employers to consider.

Top level commitment

The most useful first step an employer can take to improve the success rate of women aiming for managerial careers within an organisation is to make a conspicuous commitment to change. Some companies help by defining the values they espouse, emphasising an atmosphere of equity and equal opportunity. This needs to be supported by designated responsibilities for improving the position of women managers, monitoring systems and the active involvement of the chief executive.

To many organisations it is clear that recruiting top managers from the best people available irrespective of gender is good business. A statement to this effect from the board or the chief executive ensures that the issue is taken seriously by all managers.

British Petroleum's statement of values to its employees is:

BP

"For every employee our values mean a trusting, equal opportunity, non-discriminatory working environment. Our company offers challenging and exciting work. We will vigorously promote career development and we will aim to offer all employees a challenging career. We will seek to recognise both individual contribution and collective teamwork. We encourage our employees to strike a balance between their responsibilities to BP and to their home life".

Monitoring and auditing

Without a clear idea of where women are actually employed in the organisation it is not possible to proceed very far. A full picture enables employers to discover the possible barriers to women's career development and to define the reasons for the success of initiatives to overcome them.

Bank of England

In 1988 the Bank of England carried out a detailed analysis of the position of women and ethnic minorities in the Bank. It decided, as a result of the findings, to provide staff with equal opportunities training and to develop further its career break scheme. The analysis also confirmed that the Bank was already proceeding along the right lines with several of its policies and procedures. In its recruitment process, for example, person specifications (recruitment profiles) are used by interviewers to avoid personal, subjective judgements being made about applicants.

Enhanced maternity leave and career breaks

Initiatives in this area can be thought of as a continuum of policies, from enhanced maternity benefits and career breaks to longer, flexible career-breaks and return to work programmes.

TONY CLEAVER, CHIEF EXECUTIVE, IBM UNITED KINGDOM

"The demographic changes of the 90s and the need to attract and retain talent means that women must be enabled to achieve the most senior professional and managerial positions in companies, for their own satisfaction as well as for the success of the business.

Progressive employers will be making arrangements throughout employees' careers so that personal and family needs, including those for starting a family, may be addressed. This will enable the development of balanced and mature employees to assume both the managerial and technical leadership positions of tomorrow. In this process, the particular needs of women must not be overlooked.

I am proud of the progress that IBM has made in providing a fair and equitable working environment for all employees, but also acknowledge the challenges for further progress that employees and society in general will expect in coming years."

All women are entitled to time-off from work for ante-natal care and, provided they have worked for their employer for a minimum period, have the right to return to work. But even when a woman takes only a few weeks or months off work, practical problems may arise for employer and employee alike.

For the employee, the concern is that the job may change in her absence and that attitudes towards her in the company may alter. She will also be concerned to find good quality childcare. Employers can ensure there is someone available at work with whom women can discuss their problems without fear of prejudicing their careers.

For employers, the main concern is whether the employee will return to work. Here, keeping in touch during maternity leave seems to be of great help to both employees and employers. Care should be taken by the employer not to appear intrusive or apply pressure to return at this time.

Some organisations go further than basic advice and allow women employees longer periods of maternity leave or higher rates of pay than the law requires. Extensions to maternity leave may be attractive for some women in managerial careers. In particular, better advice and programmes to keep in touch may help women (and employers) during maternity leave.

These arrangements seem to be more common in the

public than the private sector but examples from the private sector include:

Penguin Books

Penguin Books have improved on the statutory maternity rights by halving the qualifying period for the right to return to work to one year. They also offer 25 weeks full pay for maternity leave.

Midland Bank

One of the interesting ideas developed by the Midland Bank is the Women Returner's package. This is a custom-made, open-learning package designed to help and encourage women who wish to go back to work after a career break. There are five units in the programme and subjects covered range from confidence building and stress management to assessing childcare options, and improving communication and organisational skills.

Longer career breaks are increasingly offered by employers to women employees going on maternity leave.

National Westminster Bank

The best known career break scheme is probably that of the Nat West Bank. The scheme was instituted in 1981 and substantially widened and revamped in 1989. Under the scheme, women and men are entitled to a maximum of seven years break from full time employment, as long as they undertake a minimum of two weeks paid employment each year. The career break scheme has a number of interesting features. There are career and reservist routes, the former aimed at women of high potential with the guarantee of re-entry at the original level of employment. The scheme combines access to intensive training on re-entry with the possibility of flexible working, by means of short term contracts while on a career break. The Bank will also attempt to place returners in branches at a convenient location. In June 1990, 339 women were on career breaks.

The career break scheme, although one of the more attractive solutions on offer so far, still adopts a traditional approach to management careers - a period away from work to be followed by a return to full time work. More flexible combinations of leave, part time and full time work would meet the needs of larger numbers of women and help employers to develop the talents of women who would otherwise often leave the

MICK NEWMARCH, CHIEF EXECUTIVE, PRUDENTIAL CORPORATION

"Ensuring that women managers have every opportunity to reach the very highest levels of Prudential is an important investment in our long-term future.

As one of Britain's best-known financial services groups, Prudential needs the skills that well-qualified women managers can bring to ensure we maintain our leading position into the 1990s and beyond.

We have reinforced our commitment with training courses in career development for women managers and investigated the merit of various child care schemes.

These have already begun to produce results in the form of a day care nursery for employees' children and flexible working arrangements for women managers, as well as an ever-increasing number of women who are joining Prudential as sales people, bringing their skills to help us communicate with our customers and increase business."

BP Oil

Recently BP Oil has adopted the flexible career break scheme concept. Four senior professional women at BP Oil were on the scheme in early 1990. The options are carefully discussed beforehand in individual career counselling sessions and a senior manager maintains contact with women on career breaks. The options that can be negotiated can be broken down into:

- a complete break for up to two years

- a return to office work part time

- a return to part time homeworking

- a combination of office and homeworking

- job sharing

BP Oil has also introduced a mentoring scheme for women on career breaks. A senior manager keeps in touch in order to ensure that the woman's career development is recognised and supported in her absence.

workforce. The disadvantage of greater complexity of administration cannot be ignored, but needs to be weighed against the benefits of a larger managerial pool and improved retention of skills over the longer term.

SIR BRYAN NICHOLSON, CHAIRMAN, THE POST OFFICE

"The Post Office recognises that we must support and encourage women to develop their skills to enable them to move into management positions.

Action is already being taken in key areas such as training, where a three day assertiveness course is now available, either on a women-only basis or as part of a mixed group. Promotion procedures are being revised allowing anyone with the necessary skills the opportunity to apply for promotion regardless of their current job or function. Various types of flexible working are also being introduced locally to enable people to manage their own time in agreement with their managers e.g. job-sharing, term-time working, return from maternity leave on a part-time basis. Longer term issues such as harassment, attitudes and culture are being tackled through use of internal communication, workshops and our Equal Opportunity 'Opening Doors' initiative.

There is a strong commitment to seeing that real improvements take place."

Helping with childcare

Existing policy initiatives, like longer career breaks and better maternity leave conditions, undoubtedly help women with young children return to work. A few large employers and a number of company consortia have moved to provide creches and workplace nurseries. These can be extremely useful to women with young children. But organisations should also need to consider the needs of women with school-age children. In addition, the location of workplace creches and nurseries is often a problem for families and overall costs are usually high.

Childcare is a long-term and ever changing problem and is probably the single most important reason why women fail to return to work or, having returned, fail to be promoted. A few employers do offer term time and/or part time jobs that fit around school hours. But promotion opportunities from this kind of work are virtually non-existent, as we shall see later.

School age childcare is not an insoluble problem. In the US, out of school childcare provision is commonplace. Based frequently at elementary or primary school sites, this service usually runs from 7.00 in the morning, before school starts, until 7.00 in the evening, long after school has finished. Breakfast and an evening meal are sometimes provided and parents simply pay for the hours of service they use. The Department of Education and

MICHAEL CHECKLAND, DIRECTOR GENERAL, BBC

"As a public service broadcaster, the BBC aims to provide quality programmes to suit all sections of the community. It makes sense, therefore, if the people making these programmes - the BBC's own workforce - reflect the whole community they serve. The Corporation has a very firm commitment to equality of opportunity in employment and we are constantly striving, through a very active programme of training, monitoring and targets, to do better.

The proportion of female to male staff currently employed by the BBC broadly mirrors that of the UK national labour force. But the Corporation's healthy overall percentage is weighted by large numbers of comparatively junior grade staff. We need more women in middle and senior management levels to achieve a fairer balance. Although 43 per cent of the BBC's overall workforce is female, the ratios of women to men at senior, middle and junior to middle management levels currently stand at 10:90, 18:82 and 22:78. We believe the targets we have set for 1996, of 30 per cent for women in senior management and 40 per cent for women in middle management posts are realistic and attainable by the year 1996. They will, we hope, encourage more women in broadcasting, whether already working for the Corporation or considering applying for a BBC post, to develop their full potential."

Science (DES) has recently issued guidelines requesting that schools should view positively similar initiatives organised by employers (and other bodies).

Childcare vouchers

One way employers could support childcare might be to give employees childcare vouchers. This is a relatively new concept in the UK. The idea is that employees are offered vouchers which are then used to pay for child-minders or nurseries. While they are a taxable benefit, they do not affect National Insurance contributions. Small employers, decentralised companies and those, say, in city centres where the problems of transporting children to workplace nurseries are especially difficult, might find this scheme attractive.

UK employers might also be tempted to follow the example of some of their US counterparts and introduce subsidised childcare as one of a range of "cafeteria" or self selection benefits. Employees could then choose, for example, to trade the company car against extra leave or childcare. The benefit would have to be offered to all employees, including men whose partners work for other firms. One criticism, therefore, is that vouchers subsidise other employers' workforces. But this assumes childcare is only a woman's responsibility and it also ignores the fact that many fringe benefits are enjoyed by employees, their partners and families. As long as vouchers do what all benefits are supposed to - retain and motivate talented workers - there may well be a place for them in the remuneration package.

SIR JAMES BLYTH
CHIEF EXECUTIVE,
THE BOOTS COMPANY

"Companies with the foresight to offer flexible working arrangements will continue to attract and retain the best staff. Towards the end of 1988 we introduced our innovative Term Time Working Scheme for general sales assistants. Shortly after, we became Britain's first major retailer to launch a jobshare scheme for staff at supervisory level and above. Both have proved hugely popular in a company where women make up 86 per cent of Boots The Chemists workforce.

Commitment to equal opportunities has seen the number of female store managers double in the past three years. It is now anticipated that by the year 2000 women will account for 50 per cent of all Boots store manager posts.

In the summer we launched Career Breaks, a scheme under which staff can remain in touch with their sphere of work while taking time out. Supervisory and management staff can take up to five years off without losing seniority or service, pension and holiday benefits.

When women do take the step to return to work at Boots, they can expect a full programme of retaining and updating skills. And to ensure they go back to a 'women-friendly' environment, we recently introduced training sessions for managers designed to promote the positive aspects of our equal opportunities schemes – including those for women returners."

Part time work

Part time working has been the employer's traditional response to women wanting to blend work with family responsibilities. Over 45 per cent of women in work are part timers and both marriage and children increase the tendency to part time working. The evidence is, however, that management and part time work do not go hand in hand.

According to the New Earnings Survey, a negligible number of women work part time in managerial jobs. Part time work in the building society sector has undergone a dramatic increase since 1970 yet a recent study by one researcher found that part time working cannot, at present, be combined with promotion or a career. Part time workers were found to be disadvantaged, even when compared with non-career, full time cashier staff.

The British Institute of Management survey of women managers backs up these findings. Of those women in this group with children below school-leaving age only 15 per cent worked part time. Either women managers do not choose to work part time or they feel that this is not a realistic option open to them.

But part time workers may in fact be quite ambitious. A survey of women in hospital pharmacies last year found that, apart from pay, promotion opportunities for part time staff and hours that fit domestic circumstances were the two most important factors in decisions to remain or return to work. Training was also important to these women while, perhaps surprisingly, workplace nursery provision was way down the list. Researchers also found that managers in the sector underestimated the importance to employees of promotion and help with the practical problems of re-entering the workplace.

The lessons are that career management may be just as strong a concern for part time employees as it is for other workers and that management does not always have an accurate impression of what motivates and retains their part time staff. The managerial potential of those in part time jobs is too often overlooked, as are the opportunities for part time managerial work.

Job sharing and job splitting

In an attempt to overcome the shortcomings of part time work, some employers have turned to job sharing and job splitting as a possible way forward.

Job sharing is the division of a single full time job between two people who share the responsibility, pay and benefits of the post. It is usually applied to fairly senior, responsible and skilled posts in which two sharers effectively enter a partnership. Job splitting divides jobs with less seniority, demanding less skill and little or no interaction between the two post holders. Also, job splitting is normally implemented to achieve flexibility in the labour force, or to reduce costs. In essence, the result of job splitting is indistinguishable from part time work. Job sharing, is often introduced as a reaction to internal labour market pressures and is far more likely to provide flexible work hours in high status jobs with promotion prospects for part time women workers.

Most experience of job sharing to date has been in the public sector, but even here the number of job-shares at senior levels is very small.

Boots the Chemists

Boots the Chemists has introduced a job sharing scheme aimed at supervisory levels and above. The scheme is aimed at improving retention of staff and providing them with an opportunity to fully develop their careers. It also arranges term-time working contracts which enable parents to take unpaid leave during school holidays.

Royal Borough of Kingston-Upon-Thames

All posts in the local authority, except trainee positions, are open to job sharing. The council also offers flexitime, term time working, casual work options and a dependency leave scheme that allows employees time off work to deal with urgent domestic situations.

DESMOND PITCHER, GROUP CHIEF EXECUTIVE, THE LITTLEWOODS ORGANISATION

"The Littlewoods Organisation has had a comprehensive Equal Opportunities Policy for more than 20 years. This has led to the consolidation and enhancement of the part played by women in the management and continuing success of the company.

Increasingly, we are harnessing the tremendous talents which women have to offer and reaping the benefits they bring to us. Today, we have women at every level of management up to and including our main board.

Littlewoods experience tells me that the whole of British industry can be strengthened by the growing participation of women in management."

It seems that many organisations like the sound of job sharing but have reservations about dividing jobs, especially management and supervisory posts, which employers say require continuity. Resistance to job sharing management posts or to making them available on a part time basis reflects a strong resistance to the redesign of management posts. Yet it should get easier for managers to work on both a part time and job share basis.

As the nature of work changes, the need for constant supervision declines. Much professional work relies on a manager and employee agreeing a programme of work and a deadline. The individual is then left to complete the assignment. Constant checking by a manager is unnecessary.

Interestingly, research in the National Health Service has found that health authorities with job sharing experience generally think it has fewer disadvantages than those who have yet to try the idea. For example, while 75 per cent of authorities with no job sharing experience think that part time work is unattractive to senior staff, only 35 per cent of authorities using job sharing agree.

Employers need to experiment and to question the idea that management always have to be present. Flexible hours combined with better career prospects seem to be important to women and would help to retain and motivate female staff. They can also provide a way of maintaining the skills which might otherwise be lost to the employer. Part time and job sharing management

jobs remain largely untested options. As yet they have
not been widely considered. Evidence shows that they
have also been rejected by organisations which have not
actually investigated their viability.

Homeworking

At first sight homeworking does not seem to be a viable
option for managerial work. It may, however, be an
important option for women in some types of
professional work, allowing them to continue their
careers and build up experience which may in time lead
to a management position. Companies like ICL and
Xerox, that have tried homeworking, have done so only
on a small scale, although F I Group, a computer
software house, has explored larger scale homeworking
for female computer professionals. Homeworking can
also, as we have seen, be combined with other aspects of
a flexible career break scheme.

Dual career couples

One of the issues employers will have to address in the
coming years as more women enter management, is the
mobility of couples who both work to pursue a career.
Couples may decide, as many do now, that the man's
career takes precedence. A more realistic compromise
may be that one career takes priority only some of the
time.

However, that would mean that in future employers
may be unable to assume that men move for promotion

and women don't; and it may make relocation a trickier issue than it is already. As a result, employers will have to re-evaluate their policies on management mobility. Some research has shown that mobility is often an imagined rather than a real need of corporate life.

> **_Unilever_**
>
> The consumer products multinational Unilever is tackling problems surrounding dual career mobility by operating a loosely structured dual career job search scheme. The intention is to manage the requirement for geographical mobility and respond to domestic circumstances. For example, where a partner of a relocated manager also works for Unilever, the company will try to find alternative employment for that partner at the new location. Unilever may also try to relocate employees to the same area as a spouse working for another employer.

Special management training schemes for women

Most initiatives described so far have been devised either to retain or to attract women back to work. Some, though, are geared to developing women as managers.

As noted earlier, many women workers in the UK are concentrated in jobs such as clerical or sales work, where their management potential is almost certainly overlooked. The Civil Service and at least one major bank are trying to seek out management potential in clerical grades.

The idea is to find capable clerical workers interested in progression, assess their potential and design special development programmes for the strongest management candidates. These initiatives, although still at a very early stage of development, could be a very valuable way of encouraging women whose path to promotion is blocked or where progress would normally be slow.

Midland Bank

In 1989 Midland Bank set up a one year diploma course for employees who have not had the benefit of higher education. The programme is aimed particularly at women in clerical grades and the lower management echelons who have potential but have not had the opportunity to develop it. Participants spend a year at one of five universities on a specially designed course, while receiving full salary and benefits. On their return to their workplaces they receive a full career review. In 1988–89 50 employees, including 40 women, took part in the course.

Career workshops

Another way of helping women make progress at work is to run special women-only career workshops. These have been popular in the US where the aim has been to help women challenge some of the additional barriers they have to overcome to be successful in the workplace. They also help individual women realise they are not alone in facing up to challenges at work. In this country, a number of organisations, including the Industrial Society's Pepperell Unit, run this type of workshop.

Assertiveness training is often one element of such workshops as well as sometimes being the focus of individual training. It is both a form of skill training in handling inter-personal relationships and an approach to confidence building and career development.

Prudential Corporation

The Prudential has developed a four day Career Development Course for Women, covering such areas as career and life planning, influence at meetings and assertiveness skills.

Education and training

In general, employers need to ensure that women have equal access to the training and education provided, as well as ensuring that such training does not entrench existing occupational divisions. As is noted above, less than 4 per cent of women in higher education study engineering and technology, compared to around 25 per cent of men. Men also outnumber women by a significant margin on physics based science courses.

Leicester City Council

Leicester City Council has made important strides in ensuring that women receive equal access to training. All employees of the Council can undertake qualifications training, but specific initiatives have pushed up the proportion of women undergoing training from 3 per cent in 1979 to 44 per cent in 1989. Women make up 49 per cent of the Council's workforce. Positive action is also being undertaken to increase the number of women in departments seen as male preserves, such as engineers, architects and valuers. As a result, there has been a steady increase in the representation of women at all levels of the Council.

Some employers have taken an active role in promoting scientific and technical careers to girls in schools and have supported special initiatives, like Women in Science and Engineering (WISE). Some of these initiatives have been aimed at older women with a scientific background who are considering a return to work. Others have been aimed at increasing the number of women entering fairly junior, technician-level jobs and will in time increase the numbers of women in these occupations.

British Telecom

British Telecom has run a women–only engineering access course since 1987. This course is designed to help women with an aptitude for engineering, but without the usual qualifications, to progress into higher education. The motivation for the initiative was three-fold; first, the company recognised the increasing need for graduates in engineering; second, it wanted to improve the career prospects of women employees; third, it was concerned about the gender imbalance in technical areas. It recognised that for various historical reasons women employees were less likely to have the qualifications to benefit from company higher education sponsorship schemes.

TIME FOR A RETHINK

Employers do not work in a vacuum and social changes are clearly bound to have an impact on their organisations. In the public sector, employers also have to be sensitive to the changing expectations and demands placed on them by the general public. But the commercial world does not stand still either and while social changes may affect the supply of potential managers and their aspirations, changes in the business world are likely to redefine the role of the manager and his/her job. Competitive success will depend on the ability to identify what kind of manager is needed for the 21st century and how he or she is to be groomed.

Prediction is a dangerous business, but the important issues for companies (and, to a lesser extent, for public sector organisations) during the next decade have two or three signposts.

Organisations for tomorrow's world

Adding value rather than squeezing costs is likely to become increasingly important. Product development, rapid delivery and higher quality standards are likely to supersede cost as the basis for competitive positioning.

To meet this challenge, the UK will need a flexible, multifunctional workforce guided by managers with broad experience and vision. According to management guru Peter Drucker, companies will have to move away from the command pyramid which many spent the 1950s and 1960s building, and towards flatter organisational structures, allowing for faster response to market changes and faster problem-solving.

The role of managers will also have to change. No longer will their principal role be to relay information around an unwieldy corporate colossus. Instead, middle managers are likely to group and regroup into task forces, using on each occasion their specialist knowledge to solve a specific problem or perform a specific task.

Management in the future is likely to be less about issuing orders and keeping subordinates in check and more concerned with building relationships in and outside the company. If this is so, women should prove of greater value to companies and other organisations than they already are. Their people-oriented skills should make them strong contenders for management positions in organisations far-sighted enough to acknowledge the contribution they can make.

Removing the hurdles

UK employers have made slow progress increasing the number of women in management. Well qualified women enter employment in similar numbers to men. But on the way to the top they fall in greater numbers than men at every fence. By the time employees reach junior management, only one in four is a woman and, at the most senior levels of industry, only one, possibly two, managers in a hundred is a woman. There is no one career stage at which women suddenly disappear. Their failure to reach management is a cumulative process.

Today's women managers are likely to be single and most are childless, especially if they are in senior management. Successful women managers are, therefore, a self selected population of highly career oriented survivors. Perhaps the larger groups of graduate women now moving into employment will find it easier to combine a management career with family life, but two sets of factors are likely to reduce the chances of career success, even for these highly qualified women.

First, they are likely to make career choices which do not lead to the top of the management tree, while their ambition may be under-estimated and they may be subject to selection and promotion processes which discriminate against them.

Second, they are likely to marry or have permanent relationships with men whose careers take priority, and have children. As a result, they are likely to have interrupted or part time careers for some years and to be restricted in their geographical mobility.

Nearly half the working women in the UK are employed part time. And, under current conditions, women usually have to choose between part time work and managerial careers. A recent study of BIM members concluded that there is currently an incompatibility between a career in management and bringing up children under present employment, economic and social conditions.

A commitment to equal opportunities policies for women and action to meet women's varied and changing childcare needs are fundamental to getting women back to work. How far employers go after that, however, depends on how seriously they view equal opportunities and the scale of change they are prepared to contemplate. It will also depend on their view of the benefits to be gained.

They are faced with two responses. The first, and less dramatic, broadly retains the status quo, but involves a series of piecemeal changes that improves women's ability to play the management game as it stands. The second, more challenging response, requires a radical and fundamental rethink of management careers and management development. It becomes not just a question of relaxing the rules of the game, but changing the game altogether.

The `life *is* work' approach

By simply removing some of the extra hurdles women face, employers are saying that women have to reach management the same way men do - by working continuously and full time and by fitting in their domestic responsibilities around their jobs. This traditional approach acknowledges that employers have a role to play in helping women at work gain access to management careers.

So, for example, employers encourage women to take professional qualifications or postgraduate management degrees, or make science and manufacturing careers more attractive to them. This traditional approach also includes enhancing childcare support schemes.

This approach may be the quickest short-term route to increasing the number of women managers, but it may not have the kind of dramatic results companies expect - or provide a solution to women's problems in the workplace. This is because it assumes a male way of life and working and ignores many of the social changes of the last decade. It would not, for instance, allow many women employees (and men) what they want: adequate time with their children, as well as the chance to have a fulfilling managerial career. Mature students and late starters would also go ignored because they would be too old to be considered for training and promotion. Some pace-setting companies will find this approach unsatisfactory. They will increasingly feel their way to more comprehensive solutions that satisfy the career aspirations of their female and male employees. There are already signs that some employers are taking a renewed interest in older candidates for managerial posts.

The `life *and* work' approach

This approach starts off with a change of values and a gradual movement towards integrating management careers with a positive approach to family life. It's an option that has radical consequences. It starts from the acceptance that current managerial careers often make unreasonable demands on men as well as women.

The kinds of changes employers would have to consider if they adopted this approach are:

▲ Redesigning managerial jobs to make part time and job share work realistic options.

▲ Flexible, long career break schemes with returner programmes

▲ Revising assumptions about managerial careers – are continuous employment and geographical mobility really necessary?

▲ New attitudes to age, allowing late starters and mature students entry to, and promotion in managerial careers later in life.

The way ahead

The two approaches described here are ways of making it more certain that employers will succeed if they want to utilise and develop women's management talent. The first approach removes some of the extra hurdles women face and the second brings them down in height. But in reality, these approaches are not alternatives but complementary ways of eliminating unnecessary obstacles. Helping with childcare may be a valuable aid in retaining women in the workforce but it is hard to see how they might progress up the management ranks without changes in employers' attitudes towards the developing managerial lifestyle.

Women who aspire to top management positions under present circumstances need to continue to work in the same way that men do. Their needs are not being met by improved childcare, or by career break schemes. Either their families or their employers will have to change to benefit from these initiatives. So far few employers show any sign that they are prepared to make that leap. And while they don't, many able and talented women will stay out of the workforce and out of the boardroom.

A practical approach needs to be taken, looking step by step at each and every factor affecting women's progress in management careers. The checklist which follows provides an aide memoire for organisations which wish to take advatage of the management potential of the women they employ.

A CHECKLIST FOR A CORPORATE POLICY TOWARDS WOMEN MANAGERS

This checklist is not intended to be a prescriptive statement for employers but rather to act as a comprehensive shopping list setting out the basic messages in this report. The aim is to improve the representation of women at management levels of the organisation and thus fully utilise the managerial skills and abilities of women employees.

POLICY AND PRACTICE

▲ Establish a policy aimed at improving women's opportunities to progress into management positions.

▲ Draw up a code of practice outlining the steps to be taken by the organisation, (such as job sharing, childcare help and standardised recruitment procedures).

AUDITING AND MONITORING

▲ Find out the facts by auditing the occupancy of posts at different levels of the organisation and by following the recruitment, promotion and wastage patterns of women compared to men.

▲ Periodically monitor to re-evaluate the effectiveness of the policy and measure the impact of specific initiatives.

CULTURE AND JOB DESIGN

▲ Discover how the managerial culture may impede women in the organisation. What are the unwritten codes of management?

▲ Question behaviour associated with managerial effectiveness which results in a loss of management potential. For instance, do managers have to work long hours? Is geographical mobility really essential?

▲ Carry out a functional analysis of all managerial posts. This will enable the organisation to determine what its real management needs are.

▲ Look for flexible working arrangements that match the requirements of the organisation. For example, is job sharing a possibility for certain posts?

MANAGERIAL LIFECYCLE

▲ Examine your managerial development and succession policies. Don't rule out management trainees beyond a certain age and reconsider age limits for progression.

▲ Organise career planning and counselling sessions to adjust to changes in personal circumstances and career plans.

▲ Look for ways of reducing the negative effect of maternity leave on the career progression of women managers. For example, think of flexible routes back into employment after long breaks.

▲ Unlock management potential within the organisation. Increase occupational progression and encourage late starters.

RECRUITMENT AND PROMOTION

▲ Remember that over time the increased numbers of qualified women should result in a greater proportion of women managers - keep this cohort effect in mind.

▲ Standardise all recruitment procedures to ensure fair selection. Consider the use of assessment centres, profiling and psychometric testing.

▲ Make managerial recruitment and promotion criteria clear. Do they conjure up a picture of a male manager? If so, then change them.

▲ Recruit women managers returning after a career or maternity break at a level which reflects their expertise and experience. Downward mobility after child-bearing is a typical experience of women professionals and managers.

▲ Encourage women to apply for posts by making clear that their applications will be positively viewed. Don't let the pattern of subsequent appointments suggest that this move is only cosmetic.

CAREER CHOICES

▲ Encourage women managers to make career choices that will provide the right experience for further promotion.

▲ Try to avoid occupational segregation. Women managers are often concentrated in areas such as personnel and administration which are then judged to be career 'dead-ends'

TRAINING AND DEVELOPMENT

▲ Ensure equal access to training courses. For example, women managers on career breaks should be encouraged to attend training courses.

▲ Identify potential women managers at lower levels of the organisation and nurture their development through training.

▲ Train line managers to avoid using informal, inconsistent, and unaccountable selection criteria.

▲ Offer women-only career workshops to women managers to widen their perception of their own potential, and the jobs open to them, and to increase their confidence in themselves and the organisation.

▲ Use formal mentoring programmes to support and develop women managers.

DUAL CAREER COUPLES

▲ The number of dual career couples is increasing. Be flexible in your demands for geographical mobility from all staff (male and female) in this position.

MATERNITY

▲ Be positive about maternity leave. One step is to prepare a maternity pack outlining the statutory and company benefits available. Another is to keep in touch throughout.

▲ Consider enhancing statutory maternity benefits, by lengthening the period within which women employees can return, or improving upon minimum maternity pay.

▲ Where women employees signal their intention to finish working in order to undertake childcare, consider means of attracting them back over the long term. One option is to offer a preferential reinstatement scheme.

▲ Ensure that women managers on maternity leave or otherwise absent receive details of managerial vacancies.

CAREER BREAKS

▲ Utilise career break schemes to improve the retention of women managers. Access to career break schemes can be widened or their scope increased by reducing the length of service criteria.

▲ Combine career breaks with the offer of part time and flexible working or training in order to develop and retain women managers.

CHILDCARE

▲ Consider how your organisation can help women with childcare responsibilities. Remember different women have different childcare needs. Is local childcare provision flexible and affordable?

▲ Take a flexible attitude to childcare emergencies such as illness by allowing parental leave where appropriate.

▲ Consider helping with childcare costs. One possibility is a workplace nursery or creche. Another is the establishment of holiday play and after school schemes or direct help with childcare allowances.

▲ Examine the total reward package in the organisation and how it affects existing or potential managers with childcare responsibilities. For example, can a company car or share options be traded off against childcare allowances?

▲ Consider the structure of working time the organisation operates. Can women work part time, flexitime or job share if they wish?

CARING RESPONSIBILITIES

▲ Do not assume that all women managers will necessarily have or want children.

▲ Women managers often have caring responsibilities outside work. These can include childcare, coping with sickness and looking after elderly relatives. The supply of professional careers may also decrease as more women enter the workforce. Accept this reality and adjust positively to it.

Bibliography

This bibliography sets out the major research sources used in the report. Further information on ways of improving the utilisation of women in the workforce is available from the Institute of Manpower Studies. A technical literature review containing more detailed research evidence is also available from IMS. Address: IMS, Mantell Building, University of Sussex, Falmer, Brighton, Sussex, BN1 9RF, Tel: 0273 686751.

Alban Metcalfe, B. (1984). Current career concerns of female and male managers and professionals: an analysis of free-response comments to a national survey. *Equal Opportunities International*, 3, 11–18.

Alban Metcalfe, B. (1987). Male and female managers: an analysis of biographical and self-concept data. *Work and Stress*, 1. 207–219

Alban Metcalfe, B. (1989). What motivates managers: an investigation by gender and sector of employment. *Public Administration*, 67, 95–108.

Alban Metcalfe, B. and Nicholson, N. (1989). *The Career Development of British Managers*. London: British Institute of Management Foundation.

Alston, A. (1987). *Equal Opportunities: a careers guide*. Harmondsworth: Penguin

Ashburner, L. (1989). Men Managers and Women Workers: Women employees as an underused source.

Paper presented to the Third Annual Conference of the British Academy of Management.

Atkinson, J. et al (1987). *Relocating Managers and Professional Staff*. IMS Report No. 139. University of Sussex: Institute of Manpower Studies.

Barham, K., Fraser, J. and Heath, L. (1988). *Management for the Future*. Foundation for Management Education/Ashridge Management College.

Bevan, S. and Fryatt, J. (1988). *Employee Selection in the UK*. IMS Report No. 160. University of Sussex: Institute of Manpower Studies.

Bevan, S., Buchan, J. and Hayday, S. (1989). *Women in Hospital Pharmacy*. IMS Report No. 182. University of Sussex: Institute of Manpower Studies.

British Psychological Society/Runnymede Trust. (1980). *Discriminating Fairly: a guide to fair selection*. Leicester: British Psychological Society.

Burke, R.J. and Greenglass, E.R. (1987). Work and Family. In C.L. Cooper and I.T. Robertson (Eds.). *International Review of Industrial and Organizational Psychology* 1987. Chichester: Wiley.

Campbell, R.J. and Moses, J.L. (1986). Careers from an Organizational Perspective. In D.T. Hall and Associates (eds.) *Career Development in Organizations*. San Francisco: Jossey-Bass.Green, H. (1988). Informal Careers: A study carried out on behalf of the Department of Health and

Social Security as part of the 1985 General Household Survey, Office of Population Censuses and Surveys. London: HMSO.

HMSO (1989). *Social Trends 19*. London: HMSO.

Handy, C. (1987). *The Making of Managers*. MSC/NEDC/BIM, London: NEDO

Hansard Society Commission (1990). *Women at the Top,* Hansard Society, London

Harding, N. (1989). Equal opportunities for women in the NHS: the prospects of success? *Public Administration*, 67, 51–63

Hirsh, W., Hutt, R. and Atkinson, J. (1985). *Women, Career Breaks and Re-entry*, IMS Report No. 105. University of Sussex: Institute of Manpower Studies.

Hirsh, W. and Bevan, S. (1988). *What Makes a Manager? In search of a language for Management Skills*, IMS Report No. 144. University of Sussex: Institute of Manpower Studies.

Hutt, R. (1985). *Chief Officer Profiles: Regional and District Nursing Officers*, IMS Report No. 111. University of Sussex: Institute of Manpower Studies.

Institute for Employment Research. (1989). *Review of the Economy and Employment*, Occupational Assessment 1989. University of Warwick.

Larwood, L. and Gattiker, U.E. (1986). A Comparison of the Career Paths used by Successful Women and Men. In

B.A. Cutch and L. Larwood (eds.). *Women's Career Development*, Newbury Park: Sage.

Lewis, S. and Cooper, C.L. (1989). *Career Couples*. London: Unwin Paperbacks.

MSC. (1981). *No barriers here?* A guide to career development issues in the employment of women. Sheffield: Manpower Services Commission.

Marshall, J. (1984). *Women Managers: Travellers in a Male World*. Chichester: Wiley.

Meager, N. and Metcalf, H. (1988). *Equal Opportunities Policies: Tactical issues in Implementation*, IMS Report No. 156. University of Sussex: Institute of Manpower Studies.

Meager, N. and Buchan, J. (1988). *Job-sharing and Job-splitting: Employer attitudes*. IMS Report No. 149. University of Sussex: Institute of Manpower Studies.

Meager, N., Buchan, J. and Rees, C. (1989). *Job-sharing in the National Health Service*. IMS Report No. 174. University of Sussex: Institute of Manpower Studies.

Rycroft, T. (1989). *Survey of Women Managers - Interim Report*. British Institute of Management.

Scase, R and Goffee, R. (1989). *Reluctant Managers: their work and lifestyles*, London: Unwin Hyman.

Truman, C. (1986). *Overcoming the Career Break - A Positive Approach*, Women at Work Unit, UMIST.UGC. (1989).

University Statistics 1987-88, Vol.1 Staff and Students. Cheltenham: University Statistical Record.

Waite, R. (1989). School leaver decline and the mature labour market: options and implications: In A. Harrison and J. Gretton (eds.). *Education and Training UK 1989*, Newbury: Policy Journals.

Young, K. and Spencer, L. (1990). Women Managers in Local Government: Removing the Barriers (unpublished paper).

Acknowledgments

The National Economic Development Office and the
Royal Institute of Public Administration would like to
thank the following individuals for their help in the
preparation of this report.

Kay Carberry	Trades Union Congress
John Cridland	Confederation of British Industry
Jo Gardiner	Industrial Society
Ann Greengrass	Training Agency
Dr Eleanor Macdonald	Women in Management
Pat Sloane	Management Charter Initiative
Margaret Snowden	Women in Management
Diane Stone	British Institute of Management
David Thomas	Equal Opportunities Commission
Dianah Worman	Institute of Personnel Management

We are also grateful to the staff of the companies and public
sector employers who provided the case-study material for
the report and to the business journalist Mary Bogan, who
provided additional help at the drafting stage.

Acknowledgments

The National Economic Development Office and the Royal Institute of Public Administration would like to thank the following individuals for their help in the preparation of this report.

Kay Carberry	Trades Union Congress
John Cridland	Confederation of British Industry
Jo Gardiner	Industrial Society
Ann Greengrass	Training Agency
Dr Eleanor Macdonald	Women in Management
Pat Sloane	Management Charter Initiative
Margaret Snowden	Women in Management
Diane Stone	British Institute of Management
David Thomas	Equal Opportunities Commission
Dianah Worman	Institute of Personnel Management

We are also grateful to the staff of the companies and public sector employers who provided the case-study material for the report and to the business journalist Mary Bogan, who provided additional help at the drafting stage.